Copyright©MCMLXXXI by
The C.R.Gibson Company
Norwalk, Connecticut
All rights reserved
Printed in the United States of America
ISBN: 0-8378-2028-6

*Because this page cannot accommodate all the copyright notices, the section in the back of
the book designated "Acknowledgments" constitutes an extension of the copyright page.*

A True Friend is a Gift of the Lord

Selected by Stephanie C. Oda
Illustrations by Virginia S. Thier
Designed by Bonnie Weber

The C.R. Gibson Company, Norwalk, Connecticut

These are the things I prize
    And hold of dearest worth:
Light of the sapphire skies,
Peace of the silent hills,
Shelter of the forests, comfort of the grass,
Music of birds, murmur of little rills,
Shadows of clouds that swiftly pass,
    And, after showers,
    The smell of flowers
And of the good brown earth—
And best of all, along the way,
    friendship and mirth.

Henry van Dyke

Once in an age, God sends to some of us someone who loves in us, not a false imagining, an unreal character, but looking through all our human imperfections, loves in us the divine ideal of our nature. We call this rarest of persons, who loves us not alone with emotion, but with understanding—*a friend.*

Harriet Beecher Stowe

He gain'd from Heav'n ('twas all he wished) a friend.

Thomas Gray

Mary,
I dedicate this little book
to you, for in all I read
I found you on every page
    — Love Bobbie —

Oh, the comfort—the inexpressible comfort
    of feeling safe with a person,
Having neither to weigh thoughts,
Nor measure words—but pouring them
All right out—just as they are—
Chaff and grain together—
Certain that a faithful hand will
Take and sift them—
Keep what is worth keeping—
And with the breath of kindness
Blow the rest away.

George Eliot

That friendship only is indeed genuine when two
friends, without speaking a word to each other,
can nevertheless find happiness in being together.

Georg Ebers

A slender acquaintance with the world must
convince every man that actions, not words, are
the true criterion of the attachment of friends;
and that the most liberal professions of goodwill
are very far from being the surest marks of it.

George Washington

Because of a friend, life is a little stronger, fuller, more gracious thing for the friend's existence, whether he be near or far. If the friend is close at hand, that is best; but if he is far away he still is there to think of, to wonder about, to hear from, to write to, to share life and experience with, to serve, to honor, to admire, to love.

Arthur C. Benson

I want a warm and faithful friend,
    To cheer the adverse hour;
Who ne'er to flatter will descend,
    Nor bend the knee to power;
A friend to chide me when I'm wrong,
    My inmost soul to see;
And that my friendship prove as strong
    To him as his to me.

John Quincy Adams

Behold, how good and how pleasant it is for brethren to dwell together in unity!

Ps. 133:1

A friend is a person with whom I may be sincere. Before him I may think aloud.

Ralph Waldo Emerson

Such is friendship that through it we love places and seasons; for as bright bodies emit rays to a distance, and flowers drop their sweet leaves on the ground around them, so friends impart favor even to the places where they dwell. With friends even poverty is pleasant. Words cannot express the joy which a friend imparts; they only can know who have experienced that joy. A friend is dearer than the light of heaven, for it would be better for us that the sun were extinguished than that we should be without friends.

St. John Chrysostom

Oh, I long for the glow of a kindly heart and the grasp of a friendly hand!

John Boyle O'Reilly

The making of friends,
who are real friends,
is the best token
we have of a man's
success in life.

Edward Everett Hale

Before you were my neighbor,
The woodlot was a wall
Of pink and green and silver
With blue sky over all.

But now with you beyond it,
Green arches open wide
Little doors of friendliness
Where well-worn paths divide.

With arms flung wide in welcome,
The quiet pathways smile
In happy, careless fashion
Along each shady aisle.

There is no wall between us,
Since all along the line
Are little doors of friendship
Between your house and mine.

Genieva B. Pawling

The best friend is an atmosphere
Warm with all inspirations dear,
Wherein we breathe the large, free breath
Of life that hath no taint of death.
Our friend is an unconscious part
Of every true beat of our heart;
A strength, a growth, whence we derive
God's health, that keeps the world alive.

The best friend is horizon too,
Lifting unseen things into view,
And widening every petty claim
Till lost in some sublimer aim;
Blending all barriers in the great
Infinities that round us wait.
Friendship is an eternity
Where soul with soul walks, heavenly free.

Lucy Larcom

When all at peace, two friends at ease alone
Talk out their hearts, yet still
Between the grace notes of
The voice of love
From each to each
Trembles a rarer speech,
And with its presence every pause doth fill.

Walter de la Mare

A friend is like a second self.

Cicero

I loved my friend for his gentleness, his candor, his truth, his good repute, his freedom even from my livelier manner, his calm and reasonable kindness. It was not any particular talent that attracted me to him, or anything striking whatsoever. I should say, in one word, it was his goodness. I doubt whether he ever had a conception of a tithe of the regard and respect I entertained for him; and I smile to think of the perplexity (though he never showed it) which he probably felt sometimes, at my enthusiastic expressions; for I thought him a kind of angel...With the other boys I played antics, and rioted in fantastic jests; but in his society, or whenever I thought of him, I fell into a kind of Sabbath state of bliss; and I am sure I could have died for him.

Leigh Hunt

A faithful friend is a sturdy shelter;
    he who finds one finds a treasure.
A faithful friend is beyond price,
    no sum can balance his worth.
A faithful friend is a life-saving remedy,
    such as he who fears God finds;
For he who fears God behaves accordingly,
    and his friend will be like himself.

Ecclesiasticus 6:14-17

Friendships are discovered rather than made.

Harriet Beecher Stowe

There is in friendship something of all relations, and something above them all. It is the golden thread that ties the hearts of all hearts of all the world.

John Evelyn

We cannot tell the precise moment when friendship is formed. As in filling a vessel drop by drop, there is at last a drop which makes it run over; so in a series of kindnesses there is at last one which makes the heart run over.

Samuel Johnson

To know that there are some souls, hearts and minds, here and there, who trust us and whom we trust:
Some who know us and whom we know:
Some on whom we can always rely and who always rely upon us, makes a paradise of this great world:
    This makes our life really life.

James Freeman Clarke

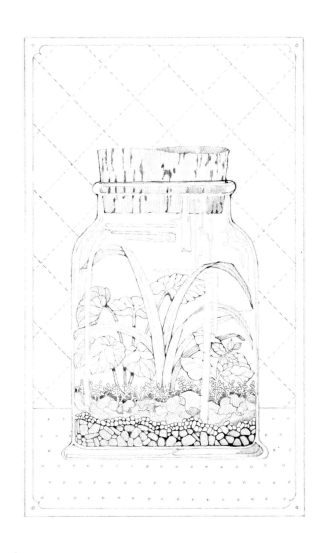

Make new friends, but keep the old,
Those are silver, these are gold;
New-made friendships, like new wine,
Age will mellow and refine.
Friendships that have stood the test—
Time and change—are surely best;
Brow may wrinkle, hair grow gray,
Friendship never knows decay,
For amid old friends, tried and true,
Once more we our youth renew.

Joseph Parry

Friendship is the nearest thing we know to
religion. God is love, and to make religion akin
to friendship is simply to give it the highest
expression conceivable by man.

John Ruskin

I am united with my friend in heart,
What matters if our place is wide apart?

Anonymous

I love you not only for what you are, but for what I am when I am with you.

I love you not only for what you have made of yourself, but for what you are making of me.

I love you because you have done more than any creed could have done to make me good, and more than any fate could have done to make me happy.

You have done it without a touch, without a word, without a sign.

You have done it by being yourself. Perhaps that is what being a friend means, after all.

Roy Croft

"Stay" is a charming word in a friend's vocabulary.

Amos Bronson Alcott

Touch but the latch, friend,
The door shall swing wide for you!

Nancy Byrd Turner

There may be moments in friendship, as in love, when silence is beyond words. The faults of our friend may be clear to us, but it is well to seem to shut our eyes to them. Friendship is usually treated by the majority of mankind as a tough and everlasting thing which will survive all manner of bad treatment. But this is an exceedingly great and foolish error; it may die in an hour of a single unwise word; its conditions of existence are that it should be dealt with delicately and tenderly, being as it is a sensible plant and not a roadside thistle. We must not expect our friend to be above humanity.

Ouida

My coat and I live comfortably together. It has assumed all my wrinkles, does not hurt me anywhere, has molded itself on my deformities, and is complacent to all my movements, and I only feel its presence because it keeps me warm. Old coats and old friends are the same thing.

Victor Hugo

I am wealthy in my friends.

Shakespeare

This life is like a garden place.
 Our friendships are the flowers,
The perfumes of the blossoms fair
 Are friendship's pleasant hours.

Mary Edith Halladay

Because we're friends, jeweled hands
At night reach from the sky,
To spread a star-dust carpet
Beneath the feet of you and I.

When morning in her golden bowl
Rides high into a smiling day,
We're friends. Thought tendrils cling
As ivy to the wall across the way.

Poet cannot write nor artist paint
The depth and beauty far expanding,
We humans call it friendship —
God calls it — understanding.

Cosmo Adele Wagner

Acknowledgments

The editor and the publisher have made every effort to trace the ownership of all copyrighted material and to secure permission from copyright holders of such material. In the event of any question arising as to the use of any material the publisher and editor, while expressing regret for inadvertent error, will be pleased to make the necessary corrections in future printings. Thanks are due to the following authors, publishers, publications and agents for permission to use the material indicated.

THE SOCIETY OF AUTHORS AND THE LITERARY TRUSTEES OF WALTER DE LA MARE, for an excerpt from *The Complete Poems of Walter de la Mare* by Walter de la Mare. Copyright (c) 1969 by The Literary Trustees of Walter de la Mare.

Photo Credits

Four By Five, Inc.—cover, pp.2,3,18,30,31; Ryan Leverkus—p.6; Kathe Gendel—pp.10,26; Steve Mack—p.11; Ed Cooper—p.15; William D. Foster—p.19; Orville Andrews—p.22; Leslie Irvin—p.27.